Dedicated to:

- All who wish to awaken their inner JOY.

- All who wish to attract more of the vibrational energy they want, into their life.

- All who wish to find appreciation in the "moments" and the "now" in their life.

<u>Other Publications by this Author:</u>
The Voyage: Finding the Beautiful Gems of My Being
The Voyage: All Age Coloring Book
Volume 1- Positive Quotes with Author Holly
30 day Gratitude/JOY Pocket Journal
Volume 2- Positive Quotes with Author Holly
90 day Daily Self-Care Accountability Logbook
90 day Daily Self-Care Accountability Log/ Reflect Journal
30 day Daily Self-Care Accountability Logbook
Volume 3- Positive Quotes with Author Holly
30 day Daily Self-Care Accountability Log/ Reflect Journal

Joyful Navigations

90 day

Gratitude/JOY

Pocket Journal

Holly Ruttenbur Dickinson

90 day Gratitude/JOY Pocket Journal
by Holly Ruttenbur Dickinson.

A 90 day Gratitude/JOY Pocket Journal .

Copyright ©2020 Holly Ruttenbur Dickinson
Joyful Navigations/Trade Name
Joyful Navigations™
Published by Shifting Open LLC.

Self-Help, Personal Growth, Happiness, Success, Motivational, Gratitude, Joy, Joyful, Journaling

Book Design, Graphics, Logbook Design by Holly Dickinson

Printed in the United States of America

All rights reserved. No portion of this publication may be reproduced, stored in a retrieval system or transmitted in any form or by any means - except for brief quotations in articles and reviews, without the prior written permission of Joyful Navigations or the Author.

Visit me on the Facebook Page: *Positive Quotes with Author Holly* and *Choose Joyful with Joyful Navigations™*
Website: https://joyfulnavigations.com

ISBN: 978-1-7355347-5-6

Table of Contents

2. Dedication, Other Titles by Holly R. Dickinson

3. Title Page

4. Copyright

5. Table of Contents

6-7. Gratitude Quotes by Author Holly R. Dickinson

8. Suggested Daily Gratitude Process

9-98. Daily Gratitude/JOY Writing Pages

99. Lined Notes Page

100. A Message from the Author

101. About the Author

Holly Ruttenbur Dickinson -Gratitude Quotes

A daily GRATITUDE journal brings me into the present moment and reminds me of all the most simple things I have to be grateful for. This is self-care. It reminds me of my JOY.

Focusing on gratitude daily, has literally rewired my brain to GO TO THE GRATITUDE. And in that gratitude, is MY JOY. It's been such a beautiful process of self discovery.

JOY and GRATITUDE are so interwoven that's it's near impossible to separate them.

When GRATITUDE is my daily practice, everything has a brighter side to it.

A daily gratitude practice isn't about denying or ignoring your other feelings and emotions or ignoring situations that need to be changed because they aren't working. Each is important to recognize and validate. A daily gratitude practice shouldn't be forced or for an external benefit accept your own well being. Willingly shifting one's focus, allows one to center on the good parts of their life, their BE-ingness. And the more JOY one receives from those simple JOYS, the more driven one can be to make the non-working parts of their life better as well.

The secret of JOY and happiness is living in a gratitude mindset.

Holly Ruttenbur Dickinson -Gratitude Quotes

Keeping a daily gratitude journal is a physical acknowledgment of conscious directional thought. We get to determine where our thoughts reside.

Choose to make gratitude and JOY your daily habits. Choose to make them your way of BEing. It is possible. It takes practice.

Back To Life:
a Gratitude Poem by Author Holly

Gratitude saved me from the depths of total grief.
Gratitude took me out of the pit of my sadness.
Gratitude reminded me how much I had to be joyful about.
Gratitude re-lit my fire within.
Gratitude walked me out of the darkness.
Gratitude saved my life.
Gratitude brought me back to life.

May you dedicate yourself to a more JOYful life through gratitude.

More gratitude, less complaining. If you don't like something, work to make it better instead. Complaining attracts more of the energy of what you don't want. Gratitude attracts more of the energy of what you want.

Suggested Gratitude Process

- Keep the pocket journal next to your bed or where you do your wake up self-care routine. Or Keep it in your day bag where it can be close to your fingertips for quick access during times of the day you know you will be able to write.

- Allow the daily practice to be a priority in order to shift your mindset to be more positive and happier. Allow your feelings in.

- No need to start at the beginning of a month. Start whenever you want throughout the month. The date is left blank for you to fill in on your schedule. The more often you do this as a daily routine, the faster it will become a healthy self-care habit. If you miss a day, that is ok. Just pick up the following day and resume the routine.

- On the "Gratitude/JOY" line, write general words. Example: Today's taxi driver.On the "Expand" lines, simply expand on your thought of why you are grateful for what you wrote as your general word/s. Example: "Grateful for today's taxi driver because she had a kind personality and was respectful. We got into a nice conversation and it helped set my day off right. I noticed that I was treating people at work kindly as well. It felt good."

Date _____   Day 1

Gratitude/JOY_____

Expand_____
_____
_____
_____
_____
_____
_____
_____
_____
_____
_____
_____
_____
_____
_____
_____
_____
_____
_____

Date _____   Day 2

Gratitude/JOY_____

Expand_____
_____
_____
_____
_____
_____
_____
_____
_____
_____
_____
_____
_____
_____
_____
_____
_____

Date _____ Day 3

Gratitude/JOY_____

Expand_____
_____
_____
_____
_____
_____
_____
_____
_____
_____
_____
_____
_____
_____
_____
_____
_____
_____
_____

Date _____ Day 4

Gratitude/JOY _____

Expand _____
_____
_____
_____
_____
_____
_____
_____
_____
_____
_____
_____
_____
_____
_____
_____
_____

Date _____ Day 5

Gratitude/JOY_____

Expand_____

_____
_____
_____
_____
_____
_____
_____
_____
_____
_____
_____
_____
_____
_____
_____
_____
_____
_____

Date _____ Day 6

Gratitude/JOY_____

Expand_____
_____
_____
_____
_____
_____
_____
_____
_____
_____
_____
_____
_____
_____
_____
_____
_____
_____

Date _____ Day 7

Gratitude/JOY_____

Expand_____
_____
_____
_____
_____
_____
_____
_____
_____
_____
_____
_____
_____
_____
_____
_____
_____
_____

Date _____ Day 8

Gratitude/JOY_____

Expand_____
_____
_____
_____
_____
_____
_____
_____
_____
_____
_____
_____
_____
_____
_____
_____
_____

Date _____ Day 9

Gratitude/JOY_____

Expand_____
_____
_____
_____
_____
_____
_____
_____
_____
_____
_____
_____
_____
_____
_____
_____
_____
_____
_____

Date _____ Day 10

Gratitude/JOY_____

Expand_____
_____
_____
_____
_____
_____
_____
_____
_____
_____
_____
_____
_____
_____
_____
_____
_____

Date _____   Day 11

Gratitude/JOY_____

Expand_____
_____
_____
_____
_____
_____
_____
_____
_____
_____
_____
_____
_____
_____
_____
_____
_____
_____
_____
_____

Date _____ Day 12

Gratitude/JOY_____

Expand_____
_____
_____
_____
_____
_____
_____
_____
_____
_____
_____
_____
_____
_____
_____
_____
_____
_____
_____
_____

Date _____ Day 13

Gratitude/JOY_____

Expand_____
_____
_____
_____
_____
_____
_____
_____
_____
_____
_____
_____
_____
_____
_____
_____
_____
_____
_____

Date _____   Day 14

Gratitude/JOY_____

Expand_____
_____
_____
_____
_____
_____
_____
_____
_____
_____
_____
_____
_____
_____
_____
_____
_____
_____

Date _____   Day 15

Gratitude/JOY_____

Expand_____
_____
_____
_____
_____
_____
_____
_____
_____
_____
_____
_____
_____
_____
_____
_____
_____
_____

Date _____ Day 16

Gratitude/JOY_____

Expand_____
_____
_____
_____
_____
_____
_____
_____
_____
_____
_____
_____
_____
_____
_____
_____
_____
_____
_____

Date _____ Day 17

Gratitude/JOY_____

Expand_____
_____
_____
_____
_____
_____
_____
_____
_____
_____
_____
_____
_____
_____
_____
_____
_____
_____
_____

Date _____   Day 18

Gratitude/JOY_____

Expand_____
_____
_____
_____
_____
_____
_____
_____
_____
_____
_____
_____
_____
_____
_____
_____
_____
_____

Date _____   Day 19

Gratitude/JOY_____

Expand_____
_____
_____
_____
_____
_____
_____
_____
_____
_____
_____
_____
_____
_____
_____
_____
_____
_____
_____

Date _____ Day 20

Gratitude/JOY_____

Expand_____
_____
_____
_____
_____
_____
_____
_____
_____
_____
_____
_____
_____
_____
_____
_____
_____
_____
_____

Date _____   Day 21

Gratitude/JOY_____

Expand_____
_____
_____
_____
_____
_____
_____
_____
_____
_____
_____
_____
_____
_____
_____
_____
_____
_____
_____

Date _____ Day 22

Gratitude/JOY_____

Expand_____
_____
_____
_____
_____
_____
_____
_____
_____
_____
_____
_____
_____
_____
_____
_____
_____
_____

Date _____ Day 23

Gratitude/JOY_____

Expand_____
_____
_____
_____
_____
_____
_____
_____
_____
_____
_____
_____
_____
_____
_____
_____
_____
_____

Date _____ Day 24

Gratitude/JOY_____

Expand_____
_____
_____
_____
_____
_____
_____
_____
_____
_____
_____
_____
_____
_____
_____
_____
_____
_____

Date _____ Day 25

Gratitude/JOY_____

Expand_____
_____
_____
_____
_____
_____
_____
_____
_____
_____
_____
_____
_____
_____
_____
_____
_____
_____

Date _____ Day 26

Gratitude/JOY_____

Expand_____
_____
_____
_____
_____
_____
_____
_____
_____
_____
_____
_____
_____
_____
_____
_____
_____
_____

Date _____ Day 27

Gratitude/JOY_____

Expand_____
_____
_____
_____
_____
_____
_____
_____
_____
_____
_____
_____
_____
_____
_____
_____
_____
_____

Date _____ Day 28

Gratitude/JOY_____

Expand_____
_____
_____
_____
_____
_____
_____
_____
_____
_____
_____
_____
_____
_____
_____
_____
_____
_____

Date _____   Day 29

Gratitude/JOY_____

Expand_____
_____
_____
_____
_____
_____
_____
_____
_____
_____
_____
_____
_____
_____
_____
_____
_____
_____

Date _____ Day 30

Gratitude/JOY_____

Expand_____
_____
_____
_____
_____
_____
_____
_____
_____
_____
_____
_____
_____
_____
_____
_____
_____
_____

Date _____ Day 31

Gratitude/JOY_____

Expand_____
_____
_____
_____
_____
_____
_____
_____
_____
_____
_____
_____
_____
_____
_____
_____
_____

Date _____ Day 32

Gratitude/JOY_____

Expand_____
_____
_____
_____
_____
_____
_____
_____
_____
_____
_____
_____
_____
_____
_____
_____
_____
_____
_____

Date _____ Day 33

Gratitude/JOY_____

Expand_____
_____
_____
_____
_____
_____
_____
_____
_____
_____
_____
_____
_____
_____
_____
_____
_____
_____
_____

Date _____ Day 34

Gratitude/JOY_____

Expand_____
_____
_____
_____
_____
_____
_____
_____
_____
_____
_____
_____
_____
_____
_____
_____
_____
_____

Date _____ Day 35

Gratitude/JOY_____

Expand_____
_____
_____
_____
_____
_____
_____
_____
_____
_____
_____
_____
_____
_____
_____
_____
_____
_____

Date _____   Day 36

Gratitude/JOY_____

Expand_____
_____
_____
_____
_____
_____
_____
_____
_____
_____
_____
_____
_____
_____
_____
_____
_____
_____
_____

Date _____ Day 37

Gratitude/JOY_____

Expand_____
_____
_____
_____
_____
_____
_____
_____
_____
_____
_____
_____
_____
_____
_____
_____
_____
_____
_____

Date _____ Day 38

Gratitude/JOY_____

Expand_____
_____
_____
_____
_____
_____
_____
_____
_____
_____
_____
_____
_____
_____
_____
_____
_____
_____

Date _____ Day 39

Gratitude/JOY_____

Expand_____
_____
_____
_____
_____
_____
_____
_____
_____
_____
_____
_____
_____
_____
_____
_____
_____
_____

Date _____ Day 40

Gratitude/JOY_____

Expand_____
_____
_____
_____
_____
_____
_____
_____
_____
_____
_____
_____
_____
_____
_____
_____
_____
_____

Date _____ Day 41

Gratitude/JOY_____

Expand_____
_____
_____
_____
_____
_____
_____
_____
_____
_____
_____
_____
_____
_____
_____
_____
_____
_____
_____

Date _____ Day 42

Gratitude/JOY_____

Expand_____
_____
_____
_____
_____
_____
_____
_____
_____
_____
_____
_____
_____
_____
_____
_____
_____
_____
_____

Date _____   Day 43

Gratitude/JOY_____

Expand_____
_____
_____
_____
_____
_____
_____
_____
_____
_____
_____
_____
_____
_____
_____
_____
_____
_____

Date _____   Day 44

Gratitude/JOY_____

Expand_____
_____
_____
_____
_____
_____
_____
_____
_____
_____
_____
_____
_____
_____
_____
_____
_____
_____
_____

Date _____   Day 45

Gratitude/JOY_____

Expand_____
_____
_____
_____
_____
_____
_____
_____
_____
_____
_____
_____
_____
_____
_____
_____
_____
_____
_____
_____

Date _____ Day 46

Gratitude/JOY_____

Expand_____
_____
_____
_____
_____
_____
_____
_____
_____
_____
_____
_____
_____
_____
_____
_____
_____
_____

Date _____ Day 47

Gratitude/JOY_____

Expand_____
_____
_____
_____
_____
_____
_____
_____
_____
_____
_____
_____
_____
_____
_____
_____
_____
_____
_____

Date _____ Day 48

Gratitude/JOY_____

Expand_____
_____
_____
_____
_____
_____
_____
_____
_____
_____
_____
_____
_____
_____
_____
_____
_____
_____

Date _____ Day 49

Gratitude/JOY_____

Expand_____

_____

_____

_____

_____

_____

_____

_____

_____

_____

_____

_____

_____

_____

_____

Date _____ Day 50

Gratitude/JOY_____

Expand_____
_____
_____
_____
_____
_____
_____
_____
_____
_____
_____
_____
_____
_____
_____
_____
_____
_____
_____

Date _____   Day 51

Gratitude/JOY_____

Expand_____
_____
_____
_____
_____
_____
_____
_____
_____
_____
_____
_____
_____
_____
_____
_____
_____
_____

Date _____ Day 52

Gratitude/JOY_____

Expand_____
_____
_____
_____
_____
_____
_____
_____
_____
_____
_____
_____
_____
_____
_____
_____
_____
_____

Date _____ Day 53

Gratitude/JOY_____

Expand_____
_____
_____
_____
_____
_____
_____
_____
_____
_____
_____
_____
_____
_____
_____
_____
_____
_____
_____
_____

Date _____ Day 54

Gratitude/JOY_____

Expand_____
_____
_____
_____
_____
_____
_____
_____
_____
_____
_____
_____
_____
_____
_____
_____
_____

Date _____ Day 55

Gratitude/JOY_____

Expand_____
_____
_____
_____
_____
_____
_____
_____
_____
_____
_____
_____
_____
_____
_____
_____
_____
_____
_____

Date _____   Day 56

Gratitude/JOY_____

Expand_____
_____
_____
_____
_____
_____
_____
_____
_____
_____
_____
_____
_____
_____
_____
_____
_____
_____
_____

Date _____ Day 57

Gratitude/JOY_____

Expand_____
_____
_____
_____
_____
_____
_____
_____
_____
_____
_____
_____
_____
_____
_____
_____
_____
_____

Date _____ Day 58

Gratitude/JOY_____

Expand_____
_____
_____
_____
_____
_____
_____
_____
_____
_____
_____
_____
_____
_____
_____
_____
_____
_____

Date _____ Day 59

Gratitude/JOY_____

Expand_____
_____
_____
_____
_____
_____
_____
_____
_____
_____
_____
_____
_____
_____
_____
_____
_____
_____
_____

Date _____   Day 60

Gratitude/JOY_____

Expand_____
_____
_____
_____
_____
_____
_____
_____
_____
_____
_____
_____
_____
_____
_____
_____
_____
_____
_____

Date _____ Day 61

Gratitude/JOY_____

Expand_____
_____
_____
_____
_____
_____
_____
_____
_____
_____
_____
_____
_____
_____
_____
_____
_____
_____

Date _____ Day 62

Gratitude/JOY_____

Expand_____
_____
_____
_____
_____
_____
_____
_____
_____
_____
_____
_____
_____
_____
_____
_____
_____
_____
_____

Date _____ Day 63

Gratitude/JOY_____

Expand_____
_____
_____
_____
_____
_____
_____
_____
_____
_____
_____
_____
_____
_____
_____
_____
_____
_____

Date _____   Day 64

Gratitude/JOY_____

Expand_____
_____
_____
_____
_____
_____
_____
_____
_____
_____
_____
_____
_____
_____
_____
_____
_____
_____

Date _____ Day 65

Gratitude/JOY_____

Expand_____
_____
_____
_____
_____
_____
_____
_____
_____
_____
_____
_____
_____
_____
_____
_____
_____
_____
_____
_____

Date _____ Day 66

Gratitude/JOY_____

Expand_____
_____
_____
_____
_____
_____
_____
_____
_____
_____
_____
_____
_____
_____
_____
_____
_____
_____

Date _____ Day 67

Gratitude/JOY_____

Expand_____
_____
_____
_____
_____
_____
_____
_____
_____
_____
_____
_____
_____
_____
_____
_____
_____
_____
_____

Date _____   Day 68

Gratitude/JOY_____

Expand_____
_____
_____
_____
_____
_____
_____
_____
_____
_____
_____
_____
_____
_____
_____
_____
_____
_____
_____

Date _____ Day 69

Gratitude/JOY_____

Expand_____
_____
_____
_____
_____
_____
_____
_____
_____
_____
_____
_____
_____
_____
_____
_____
_____
_____
_____

Date _____ Day 70

Gratitude/JOY_____

Expand_____
_____
_____
_____
_____
_____
_____
_____
_____
_____
_____
_____
_____
_____
_____
_____
_____
_____

Date _____ Day 71

Gratitude/JOY_____

Expand_____
_____
_____
_____
_____
_____
_____
_____
_____
_____
_____
_____
_____
_____
_____
_____
_____
_____
_____

Date _____ Day 72

Gratitude/JOY_____

Expand_____
_____
_____
_____
_____
_____
_____
_____
_____
_____
_____
_____
_____
_____
_____
_____
_____
_____
_____

Date _____   Day 73

Gratitude/JOY _____

Expand _____
_____
_____
_____
_____
_____
_____
_____
_____
_____
_____
_____
_____
_____
_____
_____
_____
_____

Date _____ Day 74

Gratitude/JOY_____

Expand_____
_____
_____
_____
_____
_____
_____
_____
_____
_____
_____
_____
_____
_____
_____
_____
_____
_____

Date _____ Day 75

Gratitude/JOY_____

Expand_____
_____
_____
_____
_____
_____
_____
_____
_____
_____
_____
_____
_____
_____
_____
_____
_____
_____
_____

Date _____ Day 76

Gratitude/JOY_____

Expand_____
_____
_____
_____
_____
_____
_____
_____
_____
_____
_____
_____
_____
_____
_____
_____
_____
_____

Date _____ Day 77

Gratitude/JOY_____

Expand_____
_____
_____
_____
_____
_____
_____
_____
_____
_____
_____
_____
_____
_____
_____
_____
_____
_____
_____

Date _____   Day 78

Gratitude/JOY_____

Expand_____
_____
_____
_____
_____
_____
_____
_____
_____
_____
_____
_____
_____
_____
_____
_____
_____
_____

Date _____ Day 79

Gratitude/JOY_____

Expand_____
_____
_____
_____
_____
_____
_____
_____
_____
_____
_____
_____
_____
_____
_____
_____
_____
_____
_____

Date _____   Day 80

Gratitude/JOY_____

Expand_____
_____
_____
_____
_____
_____
_____
_____
_____
_____
_____
_____
_____
_____
_____
_____
_____
_____
_____

Date _____ Day 81

Gratitude/JOY_____

Expand_____
_____
_____
_____
_____
_____
_____
_____
_____
_____
_____
_____
_____
_____
_____
_____
_____
_____
_____

Date _____ Day 82

Gratitude/JOY_____

Expand_____
_____
_____
_____
_____
_____
_____
_____
_____
_____
_____
_____
_____
_____
_____
_____
_____

Date _____ Day 83

Gratitude/JOY_____

Expand_____
_____
_____
_____
_____
_____
_____
_____
_____
_____
_____
_____
_____
_____
_____
_____
_____
_____
_____
_____

Date _____ Day 84

Gratitude/JOY_____

Expand_____
_____
_____
_____
_____
_____
_____
_____
_____
_____
_____
_____
_____
_____
_____
_____
_____
_____
_____

Date _____ Day 85

Gratitude/JOY_____

Expand_____
_____
_____
_____
_____
_____
_____
_____
_____
_____
_____
_____
_____
_____
_____
_____
_____
_____

Date _____ Day 86

Gratitude/JOY_____

Expand_____
_____
_____
_____
_____
_____
_____
_____
_____
_____
_____
_____
_____
_____
_____
_____
_____
_____

Date _____ Day 87

Gratitude/JOY_____

Expand_____
_____
_____
_____
_____
_____
_____
_____
_____
_____
_____
_____
_____
_____
_____
_____
_____
_____
_____

Date _____ Day 88

Gratitude/JOY_____

Expand_____
_____
_____
_____
_____
_____
_____
_____
_____
_____
_____
_____
_____
_____
_____
_____
_____
_____

Date _____   Day 89

Gratitude/JOY_____

Expand_____
_____
_____
_____
_____
_____
_____
_____
_____
_____
_____
_____
_____
_____
_____
_____
_____
_____
_____

Date _____ Day 90

Gratitude/JOY_____

Expand_____
_____
_____
_____
_____
_____
_____
_____
_____
_____
_____
_____
_____
_____
_____
_____
_____
_____

Notes:

A Message from the Author

Words can barely express how the daily practice of gratitude has positively altered my life. I think it would be a challenge for anyone to truly understand this until they experience the change, the shift, in their own life. I had heard that gratitude could change one's life and could attract more positive energy into one's life. I wanted to test the theory. I wanted to know if it was true. And so I took a 365 day gratitude/JOY journey. I allowed my life to be my own test subject. Within the first 30 days I began to notice more happiness and joy in my attitude and my whole being with the daily practice of gratitude. I started each day off with it and many nights I would do a second round. Imagine a year of this routine which became a very healthy self-care habit. Gratitude takes you out of "what's wrong" thinking and into "what's right" thinking in your life. May you dedicate yourself to a more JOYful life through gratitude. ~Author Holly, Your Joyful Guide.

Visit me on the Facebook Page: *Positive Quotes with Author Holly* and *Choose Joyful with Joyful Navigations*™
Website: https://joyfulnavigations.com

About the Author

Author Holly R. Dickinson is a Lightworker and a Mass Influencer of 7 million plus followers on her Facebook Page. She is a Mother of 4, now adults. She is in a loving marriage to her husband of 27 years. Early life brought many traumas and challenges to her. She shares her wisdom, perspectives, and courage in her writings. God, love, kindness, gratitude, family, awareness, courage, action, trust, compassion, forgiveness, self-care, positivity, and choosing joy are key for her.

www.ingramcontent.com/pod-product-compliance
Lightning Source LLC
LaVergne TN
LVHW020936090426
835512LV00020B/3392

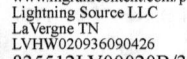